BESIDE THE SEASIDE

SEASIDE PLANTS AND ANIMALS

Clare Hibbert

W
FRANKLIN WATTS
LONDON • SYDNEY

First published in 2015 by
Franklin Watts
338 Euston Road
London NW1 3BH

Franklin Watts Australia
Level 17/207 Kent Street
Sydney NSW 2000

© 2015 Franklin Watts

ISBN 978 1 4451 3766 7
Library eBook ISBN 978 1 4451 3768 1

Dewey classification number: 578.7'699

A CIP catalogue record for this publication is available from the
British Library.

Planning and production by Discovery Books Limited
Managing editor: Paul Humphrey
Editor and picture researcher: Clare Hibbert
Design: sprout.uk.com

Printed in China

Franklin Watts is a division of Hachette Children's Books,
an Hachette UK company.
www.hachette.co.uk

Photo acknowledgements: **Alamy**: 4b (Neil Smith), 12 (Keith
Taylor), 17t (Dave McAleavy Images); **Bigstock**: 9t (Johan
Larson), 19b (Whiskybottle), 22 (Jeni Foto); **Corbis**: 17b (Stuart
Black/Robert Harding World Imagery); **Discovery Picture
Library**: 8 (Chris Fairclough); **Shutterstock**: beachball
art (Virinaflora), word box hut (AnastasiaN), seaside icons
(Aleksandra Novakovic), heading strips (Inna Ogando), cover
and title page (Mighty Sequoia Studio), 3 background
(Alan Bryant), 4c (Paul Nash), 5 (jaroslava V), 6l (TTphoto),
6r (Martin Fowler), 7 (V Belov), 9b (Tomek Friedrich), 10 (Philip
Bird), 11 (Gertjan Hooijer), 13 (davidpstephens), 14 (Cheryl
Casey), 15 (Kuttelvaserova Stuchelova), 16 (Bildagentur Zoonar
GmbH), 18l (LianeM), 18r (krcil), 19t (Bildagentur Zoonar
GmbH), 20 (Gerald Marella), 21 (Bildagentur Zoonar GmbH);
sprout.uk.com: bucket and spade art.

Find it!
As you read this book, look out for hidden buckets and spades. There are nine to spot.

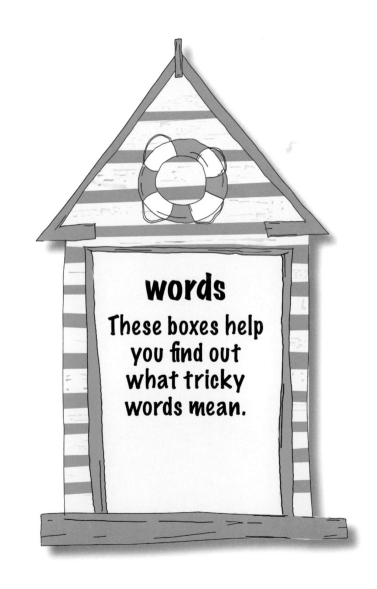

words
These boxes help you find out what tricky words mean.

CONTENTS

At the seaside **4**

Among the seaweed **6**

Rock pools **8**

Stars and flowers **10**

Crabs and lobsters **12**

All kinds of shells **14**

A sandy home **16**

On the cliffs **18**

Offshore visitors **20**

Things to do **22**

Notes for adults **23**

Index **24**

AT THE SEASIDE

The seaside habitat changes all the time. At high tide, seawater floods the beach. Strong, salty winds blow in from the sea and over the cliffs.

Plants and animals that live by the sea have to be tough to survive. They include wiry grasses on the dunes and slimy seaweeds on the rocks. There are wriggling lugworms and armour-plated crabs.

Squawk!

habitat

The place where an animal or plant lives.

There is a lot of busy bird life. One of the first things you notice is the sound of the seabirds. Kittiwakes and other gulls call to each other as they swoop for fish. They squawk as they pick over shells on the rocks or when they are begging for a bite of your picnic!

AMONG THE SEAWEED

Seaweeds are algae and look a bit like plants. You find them in the salty sea. Unlike plants, they don't have roots, stems or flowers.

Seaweeds cling to underwater rocks or float in the water. Some types have little air pockets that help them to float. Seaweeds make a good hiding place for small, darting fish. Tiny snails called periwinkles live and feed on the seaweed, too.

air pocket

At low tide, oystercatchers (above) and other wading birds come and feed on the tiny creatures on the seaweed.

alga (plural: algae)
A plant-like living thing that grows in water, with no true stems or leaves.

ROCK POOLS

Rock pools are amazing habitats on rocky shores. Next time you see one, investigate how many seaweeds and animals it has. Look for tiny crabs and squishy starfish!

A rock pool is a difficult place to live. At low tide, the water heats up in the sun. **Predators** can easily fish out animals from the pool. At high tide, the creatures risk being washed away.

Hey! Look at this little fish!

Rock-pool animals have ways of surviving. Some burrow into the sandy bottom of the pool. Others grip the rocks and clamp their shells shut. Barnacles have a shell of plates that close tight at low tide (top picture). At high tide, the plates open so the barnacles can feed (bottom picture).

predator
An animal that hunts and eats other animals for food.

STARS AND FLOWERS

Two of the most amazing rock-pool animals can change their shapes. Anemones can look like flowers or slimy balls. Starfish stretch or squash their many-armed bodies to fit their hiding places.

Starfish hide between rocks at low tide. At high tide, they come out to eat. Mussels are a favourite food. Starfish wrap their body around the mussel and pull apart its two shells. Then they stick part of their stomach next to the soft bit of the mussel and **digest** it!

Anemones are sea creatures in the same family as jellyfish. They are predators. Their pretty 'petals' (top picture) are deadly, stinging tentacles. The anemone uses its tentacles to catch shrimps, worms and baby fish. At low tide, the anemone pulls in its tentacles and looks like a slimy blob (bottom picture)!

digest
To break food down so the body can take it in.

CRABS AND LOBSTERS

Crabs of many sizes live in rock pools. Pea crabs are no bigger than a pea. Shore crabs can be nearly 10 cm across.

Crabs are scavengers. They scuttle across rock pools or the seabed and clear away old, rotting material by eating it up. A lump of rotting fish is a feast for a crab! Crabs, in turn, are eaten by seagulls.

You might find empty crab shells on the beach. Some were left by gulls, but others were shed by crabs as they grew.

Crabs are part of the **crustacean** family, along with their cousins, lobsters. Lobsters live in the sea and do not scavenge. They prefer fresh food.

crustacean

An animal with a segmented body covered by a hard outer case, and jointed legs with two parts.

ALL KINDS OF SHELLS

Do you like collecting empty shells at the beach? Some of these wash up from the sea. Others come from rock pools. Each shell once protected an animal's soft body.

Most shells protect creatures called **molluscs**. Snails are part of the mollusc family. They have a spiral shell. Whelks and periwinkles have a single, spiral shell, too. They are known as sea snails.

How many shells have you found?

Some molluscs have a pair of shells that are hinged so they can open up or snap shut. There are wedge-shaped mussels (left) and long, thin razor shells, as well as cockles, clams and oysters. All these molluscs, or shellfish, are good to eat. People collect them from the rocks at low tide.

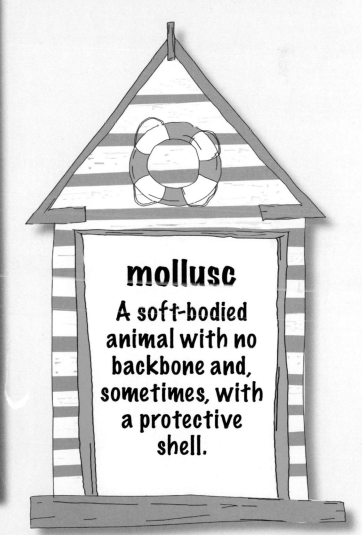

mollusc

A soft-bodied animal with no backbone and, sometimes, with a protective shell.

A SANDY HOME

Compared to rocky shores, with their rock pools full of life, sandy beaches seem bare. Take a closer look! You will find many interesting minibeasts living there.

The tide washes up kelp and other seaweed on the beach, which soon swarms with kelp flies and tiny red mites. Sandhoppers hop along the sand or burrow beneath it. Lugworms and ragworms live under the sand, too. You can tell where their burrows are by the curly **casts** they leave at the surface.

casts

cast
A tube-shaped coil of sand that has passed through a lugworm's body as it made its burrow.

Some beaches have dunes – mounds of sand at the top of the beach where tough marram grass grows. Rabbits live among the sheltered dunes and shelducks may nest there. Some dunes are even home to rare sand lizards (above).

ON THE CLIFFS

Kittiwakes and other kinds of seagull nest in the craggy cliffs. They lay their eggs on narrow ledges, out of reach of predators. Puffins (below, right) raise their chicks on cliff tops, too.

The top of the cliff is a tough place to live. It is whipped by the wind. Grass and scrubby plants such as gorse, heather and tasty rock samphire grow on the cliff top. There are brambles and dog roses, thrift, sea holly and spurge. Sometimes farmers graze **hardy** sheep or cattle.

Chalk cliff tops are home to spider orchids (right), which need chalky soil. They get their name because the flowers look a bit like spiders. These plants attract bees, while other flowers attract butterflies (below).

hardy

Able to cope with tough conditions.

OFFSHORE VISITORS

There is a great view of the sea from the top of the cliffs. You may see some surprising visitors swimming near to the shore.

Basking sharks – one of the largest kinds of fish – feed near the surface. They cruise around the coast with their huge mouths gaping wide, ready to scoop up a meal.

You might spot dolphins (left) or porpoises leaping from the water. Unlike fish, dolphins and porpoises cannot breathe underwater. They come to the surface to take in air.

Seals need to come up to breathe, too. Unlike dolphins and porpoises, they can leave the sea. They **bask** on the rocks and have their pups on the shore.

bask

To warm up in the sun. Basking sharks get their name because of being seen in the warmer water near the surface.

THINGS TO DO

Now you've found out lots about seaside plants and animals. Are you ready for a project? Here are some ideas for fantastic follow-on activities:

1. Create a seaweed mobile

Ask an adult to twist together two wire coathangers to make the mobile. Use brown, green and red crêpe paper to make long trails of seaweed: strap-like brown and green kelp, feathery red seaweed and lumpy bladderwrack. Tape them to your mobile.

2. Taste some seafood

When you have the chance, try some seafood. Mussels are fun – you can use the first empty pair of shells as pincers to eat the rest! Or do a blindfolded taste test – can you tell a whelk from a cockle? If you don't eat shellfish, try seaweeds instead.

3. Move like a seaside animal

Why don't you experiment with moving your body in different ways? Flap your wings like a gull, dart and shimmy like a fish, scuttle like a crab or wriggle like a lugworm!

4. Make a rock pool mural

On a big piece of card, sketch a pool in cross section full of animals and seaweed. Experiment with painting techniques – for speckled rocks, flick your loaded brush.

5. Have fun with shells

Collect shells whenever you can. You can do lots with them. Place one by your ear – can you hear the sea? Order them by size or texture. How many can you identify? Get crafty with them – press them into clay or use them as stampers for printing.

NOTES FOR ADULTS

The **Beside the Seaside** series has been carefully planned to provide an extra resource for young children, both at school and at home. It supports and extends their learning by linking to the KS1 curriculum and beyond.

In Geography, a foundation subject at this level, the seaside is a rich and popular topic because it allows children to:

1a Ask geographical questions [for example, 'What is it like to live in this place?']

1c Express their own views about people, places and environments [for example, residents and tourists, resort attractions and places to stay]

2a Use geographical vocabulary [for example, near, far, north, south, coast, cliff]

2d Use secondary sources of information [for example, books, pictures, photographs, stories, information texts, videos, artefacts]

3a Identify and describe what places are like [for example, in terms of landscape, jobs, weather]

3c Recognise how places have become the way they are and how they are changing [for example, the importance of the fishing industry]

3d Recognise how places compare with other places [for example, compare a seaside town to a city. 4a Make observations about where things are located [for example, a bandstand on a pier or in a public park] and about other features in the environment [for example, seasonal changes in weather]

It also provides plenty of opportunities for crossover work with other subjects.

The four titles in this series split the seaside into four sub-topics:
Seaside Holidays Now and Then
Seaside Jobs
Seaside Plants and Animals
Seaside Towns

In addition to Geography, the four books support the core subjects of English, Mathematics and Science and other foundation subjects such as Art and Design, Design and Technology and History – especially if children are encouraged to get involved in the suggested extension activities on the facing page.

Reading with children

When children are learning to read, they become more confident and make quicker progress if they are exposed to as many different types of writing as possible. In particular, their reading should not only focus on fiction and stories, but on non-fiction too. The **Beside the Seaside** books offer young readers different levels of text – for example, straightforward factual sentences and fun speech bubbles. As well as maintaining children's interest, these offer children the opportunity to distinguish between different types of communication.

Make the most of your reading time. Whether it is the adult or the child who is reading, he or she should try to follow the words with his or her fingers – this is useful for non-readers, reluctant readers and confident readers alike. Pausing in your reading gives a chance for questions and to discuss the content of the pictures. For reluctant readers, try turning the reading into a game – perhaps you read alternate pages, or the child only reads speech bubble text. To further encourage interactivity with the content, there is a small artwork of a bucket and spade hidden on every main spread for children to find.

INDEX

A

algae 6–7
anemones 10–11

B

barnacles 9
basking sharks 20–21

C

clams 15
cliffs 4, 18–19, 20
cockles 15
crabs 4, 8, 12–13
crustaceans 12–13

D

dolphins 20–21
dunes 4, 17

F

fish 5, 6, 8, 11, 12, 20

G

grasses 4, 17, 18
gulls 5, 12, 18

H

habitats 4, 5, 8
heather 18

K

kelp flies 16
kittiwakes 5, 18

L

lobsters 13
lugworms 4, 16

M

molluscs 14, 15
mussels 10, 15

O

oystercatchers 7
oysters 15

P

periwinkles 6, 14
porpoises 20–21
predators 8, 9, 11, 18
puffins 18

R

rabbits 17
razor shells 15
red mites 16
rock pools 8–9, 10, 12, 14, 16

S

samphire 18
sand lizards 17
sandhoppers 16
scavengers 12
sea holly 18
seals 21
seaweeds 4, 6–7, 8, 16
shelducks 17
shells 5, 9, 10, 12, 14–15
spider orchids 19
spurge 18
starfish 8, 10

T

tides 4, 7, 8–9, 10, 11, 15, 16

W

whelks 14